I0159646

Oscar Micheaux

A Self-Made Man

Second Edition

By Jeremy Geltzer

Also by Jeremy Geltzer
Behind the Scenes: a Child's Guide to Film History
Charlie's Little Tramp
Latino Hollywood
Race Films: 50 Years of Independent African American Cinema

Oscar Micheaux A Self-Made Man © The Hollywood Press, 2013

Published by the Hollywood Press
hollywood-press.com
First Edition, September 2013
Second Edition, August 2015

Introduction

What was the first movie you ever saw? What is your favorite movie? Has a movie ever made you cry?

Movies can make us laugh or reach for a hand to squeeze because we're scared. We see movies when we are out with our friends. And when we're alone we can be star in our own dream-movies.

But stories from behind the scenes can be as interesting as the movies. The lives of screen stars tell tales of people who followed their dreams. People who strived for success against the odds. Some of their stories may be familiar—like Charlie Chaplin's little tramp and Judy Garland's trip over the rainbow to Oz. Others may be less familiar, like Oscar Micheaux's passion for books and film or the Lumière brother's magical invention.

Behind the Scenes tells the stories of how the movies were made. The lives of the stars that made history can be as exciting and inspiring as the movies they were in. *Behind the Scenes* opens a door to movie history reminds us to believe in our dreams.

Oscar Micheaux
A Self-Made Man

A sea of green sped by outside the window. Leafy crops sprouted from dark rich soil as a train engine chugged through the farmland of the Mississippi delta. Cotton, corn and sugarcane grew on both sides of the train tracks. Every few miles small groups of children gathered to watch the locomotive.

The engineer tooted his whistle as the children waved. The train was long with maybe 30 cars trailing behind the engine. It was a fun show and a nice break from the hot muggy summertime.

On the train, passengers watched the beautiful landscape pass outside the windows of the Pullman cars. The Pullman Palace Car was where the richest men on the train would gather. In the Palace car the seats were cushy red velvet. The floors were hardwood. Curtains hung above the windows to make the compartment look like a royal hall. At one end of the car a sign hung

Inside a luxury Pullman Railway Compartment

that read: "Travel and Sleep in Safety and Comfort." The sign swayed ever so slightly from the motion of the train. Beneath the sign was a small space where the Pullman porters kept their supplies. Here a young man sat organizing his toolbox.

"Hey Oscar," said a tall African American man walking down the aisle clicking his hole-puncher. He seemed friendly as he greeted the young man at his toolbox.

The young man looked up. "Hello George," said Oscar. George was dressed fine. He wore a square-shaped hat with a little brim. Just above the brim was a bronze plaque that read "Pullman Porter." He wore a wool jacket with shiny brass buttons. Three golden stripes sparkled on his sleeve. George had been a Pullman Porter for many years. He knew the railroad well—he had been from Chicago to New Orleans more times than he could count. He knew many of the passengers and they knew him.

"Oscar, it looks like we got some high rollers in the cabin. You might want to hurry up your organizing and get out there to shine some shoes before someone else does the job. These guys will give good tips, I tell you."

"I'm on it right now! Thanks for looking out for me, George. I just like keeping my gear in order." Oscar stood up. He was tall and slim and handsome. Although he lacked the golden thread that George wore, Oscar was still impressive. He took off down the compartment with his toolbox.

In the passenger car the Thibodaux brothers stretched out on comfy chairs. Although Henry, Emil, Bartholomew and Norbert ran their father's plantation, their hands were soft and pink. They didn't do much of the hard work themselves. Henry turned a silver dollar coin over and over in his hand. A newspaper sat unread in his lap. Bartholomew and Norbert played cards. Both boys were cheating. Emil looked out the window.

"Excuse me, gentlemen," Oscar cleared his throat and spoke in a clear voice. "Can I interest any of you in a shoeshine? Best shine South of the Mason-Dixon Line. Then once we cross, I'm the best in the North." He smiled warmly.

Bartholomew and Norbert ignored him. Henry glared with angry eyes and continued to turn the coin over and over in his hand. Oscar stood there confidently. He He kept on smiling. He held his toolbox steady. The landscape whizzed by outside the window.

Emil looked down at his boots and rubbed the toe with his finger. Then he turned to Oscar. "Why, yes. Yes I do think that I need a fresh polish."

Oscar's smile stretched wider as he sat down on a stool and Emil placed a boot on the corner of Oscar's toolbox. Oscar snapped his rag got right to work. He brushed and buffed and smeared polish on the shoe and shined it up. The old boot looked new again.

"I'm ready for your other shoe, sir." Oscar said politely.

"That sure is a nice job," Emil remarked. "What's your name, shoeshine boy?"

"Oscar, sir. Oscar Micheaux."

"Micheaux. That sounds French. I like it. How did you come by a French name?"

"My granddaddy was born a slave in Kentucky. The plantation owner was a Frenchman. After the War Between the States, I guess my daddy just took the name of the slave owner as his own. Me, I was born in Metropolis, Illinois. Not that far from that old plantation in terms of distance as the crow flies, but a whole different world anyhow. I was born a free man."

"You have an interesting story, Oscar. How did you come to be a Pullman porter?"

"Oh this is a right sweet job. I get to travel. I make money—I save my money. I even get myself an education by talking to worldly customers such as yourself." He gave a dramatic flourish with his shining cloth and snapped it in the air again. "And I do work for tips, you know."

"I like you Oscar. You have gumption. You know what that is? It's the courage to take action. It's common sense and guts. You might have guessed what I do. My brothers and I run our daddy's plantation. I got a tip for you. Land. Buy land. Get yourself forty acres and a mule. They're not making any more land, so buy up what you can. The big farms own the South, so you might want to look North. Hey Henry, toss me your newspaper. You're not reading it."

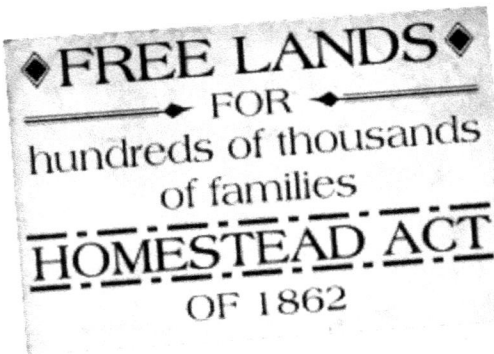

♦FREE LANDS♦
— ► FOR ◄——
hundreds of thousands of families
HOMESTEAD ACT
OF 1862

Henry frowned. He flipped the coin over in his hand. Then he picked the paper up, folded and tossed it across the aisle to Emil.

"Thanks. Yes, see here." Emil pointed to the newspaper. "In the North, the far North, the government is pretty much giving land away to homesteaders. There aren't enough people up there and Dakota just became a state. They need people and money." Emil smiled at his shiny shoes.

He looked back at Oscar and continued. "Go where there aren't enough people and make yourself some money. That's my tip."

Oscar's grin drooped just a bit.

"Oh, don't worry Oscar, that's not my only tip. Henry, let me see your coin."

Henry flipped the coin across the aisle to Emil.

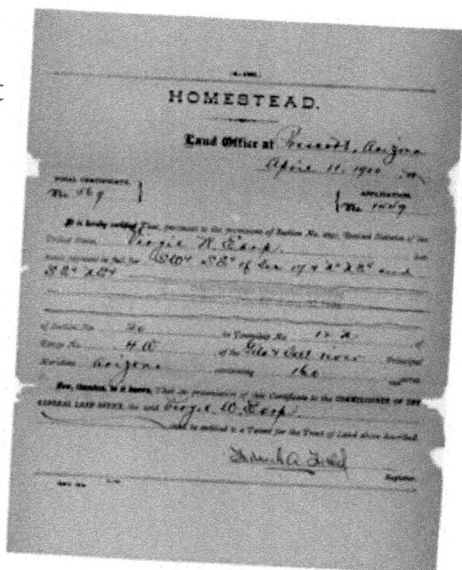

"Thanks. Here you go Oscar."

"A dollar!?" The coin gleamed in Oscar's palm. " Thank you sir!"

"Remember what I said."

"Oh, I will. Thank you!"

Oscar sat on an uncomfortable train seat looking out the window. This landscape had no color at all. All he saw in every direction was a dusty, dusky beige-ish brown. His suitcase sat on the floor in front of him. The train was nearly empty.

Oscar was headed into South Dakota where the U.S. Government was selling land cheap. But Dakota Territory was far different from the quiet farmland of the South or bustle of Chicago, which Oscar had grown used to. Dakota was home to the badlands and filled with towns with names like Deadwood, Spearfish and Wounded Knee. The train screeched into a station. A peeling, weathered sign read: "Bonesteel." Oscar picked up his bag and walked to the door.

The town seemed to be made out of splintery wood. One building had a sign out front that read "U.S. Government outpost." When Oscar stepped through the swinging doors everyone stopped talking. All the heads in the room turned towards him. Everyone was white. It was like they had never seen an African American man before. Maybe many of them hadn't.

Oscar stepped up to the counter. "I'd like to purchase some land."

"You got money?" snorted a man with a gray hat who stood behind metal bars.

"Yes, sir."

"You ever taken up arms against the United States Government?"

"No sir."

"You ever been to jail?"

"No."

"You twenty-one years of age?" He coughed into a yellow handkerchief.

"Um. Yep." This wasn't really true. Oscar was not yet twenty-one years old.

"Allllllllllllrighty then." The man took out a map of the territory. He raised his meaty hand and pointed one thick dirty finger. The finger came down on the map with a thwack. "Right here is a solid spot. Decent dirt. Fresh water. Southwest corner of the southwest quarter of section 29 township, range seventy-two west of the fifth principal meridian."

Oscar had no idea what he was talking about.

"Them's the directions. One hundred and sixty bucks. Cash only."

"One hundred and sixty bucks." Oscar smiled. "Forty acres and a mule."

"Forty? Heck. A hundred and sixty bucks buys you a hundred and sixty acres in these parts. You're on your own about the mule, though. You can probably buy one in town.   General Store is pretty well stocked with whatnot." Oscar took out a leather bag and counted out one hundred and sixty dollars as everyone watched. He signed his name to the deed. Oscar was now a homesteader.

A homestead in South Dakota, 1910

The winter winds howled across the Great Plains.

Oscar took shelter in his homestead. His harvest had been decent. He had enough food to live and grew enough extra to sell and trade. He was even able to save some money. But when you are a homesteader, you have to do everything yourself. Food had to be prepared, dried, smoked or pickled. Clothing had to be mended, darned or patched. Shelter needed to be fixed, maintained or refinished. It was a lot of work. Oscar liked doing work. But there was also a lot of waiting. Waiting for the rain to come. Waiting for the food to grow. Oscar did not like waiting.

During the cold, damp months, a lantern burned in Micheaux's one room shack. The homesteader sat at a desk that he had made himself on a chair that he made himself. His hands stayed busy. His hands had planted and harvested his crops. His hands had built and repaired his house. Now his hands were writing. As everyone else settled down for the long winter season, Oscar dove into a new project. He was writing a book.

The book was about an African American man who purchased land in Dakota Territory as he tried to better his life. As Oscar finished the last chapter, he named the story "The Conquest, the story of a Pioneer." He got to work on a second book called "The Homesteader." Both books told the realistic story about how hard life could be, but the message was that a man or woman could achieve success if he put his or her mind to the task at hand and worked through it. Oscar published his books and was happy to see that people bought and read it.

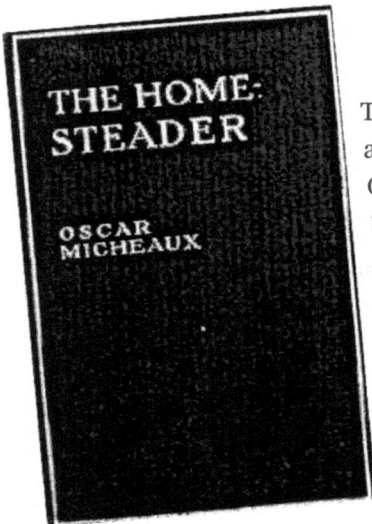

THE HOME-
STEADER

OSCAR
MICHEAUX

Two books written and published by Oscar Micheaux: *The Conquest* in 1913 and *The Homesteader* in 1917

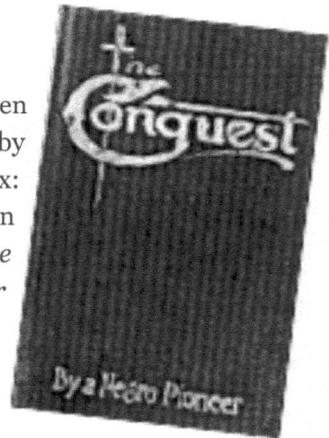

Once day he received
a telegram:

WESTERN UNION TELEGRAPH

To: Mr. Micheaux – stop –
Enjoyed reading your book The Homesteader
– stop –
We are interested in making it into a movie
– stop –
We plan on visiting Dakota in 6 weeks time
and would like to call on you – stop –
Signed,
The Johnson Brothers, George & Noble
– stop –

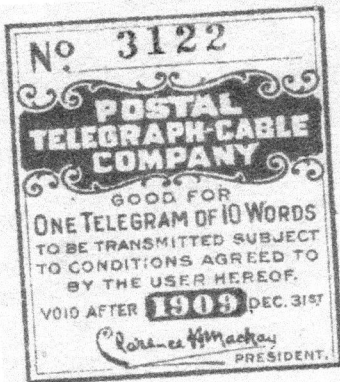

Six weeks later there was a
knock on Oscar's door.
When he opened it two well-
dressed African American
men stood on the porch.
The smaller man wore horn-
rimmed glasses. The other
man was massive—over six

Oscar could see muscles rippling through his clothes. The giant man's eyes glared intensely.

The horn-rimmed glasses man smiled. "Hello, Mr. Micheaux? We represent the Lincoln Motion Picture Company. We sent you a telegram regarding your novel, "The Homesteader." We'd like to purchase the rights to make a movie."

Noble (left) and George Johnson

Oscar invited the two men in. Their names were George and Noble Johnson. Noble was the giant. The Johnson brothers had opened their own movie studio in California. George explained that they wanted to present positive images of African Americans. They wanted to help elevate black communities around the country. Noble was the small studio's star. He also acted in other films—Hollywood films—but his passion was to play righteous black characters that African American children could look up to.

Oscar was interested in their story. They had been making movies for four years and were one of the first all-black film studios. There was a group of theaters, mostly in the Southern States, that played all-black films to all-black audiences. These theaters needed movies with encouraging messages. It was good for the community. "And a good way to make some money," George smiled. Noble did not smile.

THE TROOPER OF TROOP K
IN 3 PARTS

Featuring
NOBLE M. JOHNSON
SUPPORTED BY
BEULAH HALL AND JIMMIE SMITH
A THRILLING PICTURIZATION OF THE LATE
CARRIZAL,MEXICO BATTLE,BETWEEN THE FIGHTING
U.S.TENTH CAVALRY AND THE CARRANZISTAS SOLDIERS
LINCOLN MOTION PICTURE COMPANY
LOS ANGELES. CALIF.

Oscar listened to the Johnson brothers but his mind was working faster than they were talking. Yes, Oscar would make "The Homesteader" into a movie. Yes, he would bring its encouraging message about a self-made man's success to the screen. This was a story of hope that African American audiences needed to hear.

But no, he would not do it with the Johnson brothers. Oscar would do it himself.

Oscar sold his land in Dakota and hopped aboard a train heading to Chicago. He was ready to start making his movie but didn't know where to begin. Walking down the city streets, Oscar stepped into a diner to eat a meal and think about his plan.

"Hiya honey," a sweet voice said. Oscar turned. A girl was talking to him. "You're new in town, country boy."

Oscar realized that he was still wearing his farming clothes. There was still mud on his boots and Dakota dust in his hair.

Oscar smiled his warm smile and spoke. "I've traveled from New Orleans, Louisiana to Bonesteel South Dakota, but I have finally arrived back where I started in sweet home Chicago. I've shined shoes, planted crops and written books. But I am here to make a movie. I'm gonna make history."

"Can I start you off with a hamburger?"

Evelyn Preer

"What's your name?"

"Evelyn"

"Evelyn, what?"

"Evelyn Preer."

"Do you want to be a movie star Evelyn Preer?"

Oscar and Evelyn became fast friends. She took him out to buy a new set of clothes. By the end of the day, the dusty, muddy-shoed homesteader had disappeared. Now, Oscar looked at his reflection in a full-length mirror. He wore a herringbone seersucker suit, black patent leather shoes and a pocket watch with a fob. He had a white hanky in his pocket and a golden ring on his finger. Evelyn smiled at him. "You need one more thing." She picked out a stylish fedora and walked over to him. She stood on her tippy toes to place the hat on his head. Oscar looked back in the mirror and winked.

"The Car of 1918"

Oscar had enough money to pay for his clothes. He had plenty of money still to buy Evelyn a stylish gown and a pearl necklace. They even bought a brand new 1918 Ford Model T automobile. He had saved enough money to pay for it all. But he did not have enough money to make the movie. Evelyn asked him if he had a plan.

Oscar Micheaux

"My plan has three parts." Oscar said. "Part one is to look real fine, like we're respectable people."

"Mission accomplished," said Evelyn.

"Part two is to sell the movie."

"But you haven't made the movie."

"That's a minor detail."

"It's not so minor, Oscar. How are you going to sell something that you don't have?"

"Oh we're gonna have it."

"Then where is it?"

"We gotta sell it first."

"Oscar," Evelyn's head was spinning. "How are you gonna sell something that you don't have? How are you gonna sell something that doesn't exist?"

"With this." Oscar pointed to his smile.

"You're going to sell a make-believe movie with your smile?"

"With this." Oscar pointed to his smile.

"You're going to sell a make-believe movie with your smile?"

"And this," he motioned to his new outfit.

"Still not seeing how this is going to work."

"And this," Oscar tapped on the cover of his book, "The Homesteader." Here's my plan. We sell the film to theaters—exclusive first run rights to show the blockbuster movie based on the best selling novel by Oscar Micheaux. Then once we collect the money, we use that for part three."

"What's part three?"

"Make the film!"

"Oscar you're crazy," Evelyn smiled at him. "Crazy like a fox."

And that's exactly what Oscar Micheaux did. Wearing a fine suit of clothes, he drove around the Midwest and Southern States pre-selling his movie. In those days there were special theaters for black only audiences. They had black musicians, black singers, black comedians and sometimes black movies. These theaters were called the Chitlin Circuit. Oscar traveled along the Chitlin Circuit shaking hands, giving away copies of his book and collecting pre-paid bookings for his film. Once he had the cash in hand, he returned to Chicago and started filming the story with Evelyn. His finished his first film, *The Homesteader*, in 1919. The film was a hit with African American audiences.

He got right to work on his next film, *The Symbol of the Unconquered*

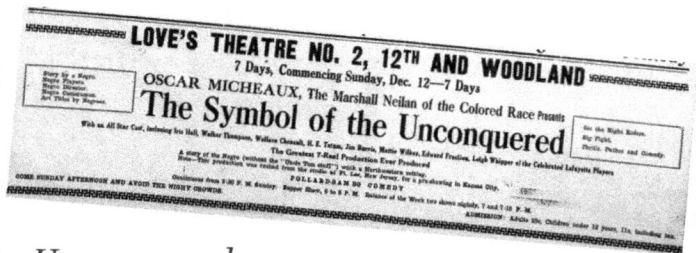

(1920). Once again Oscar pre-sold the booking dates until he had enough money to make the film. Then he drove around from theater to theater with the movie. He loved working, raising money, making movies and showing them to audiences not used to seeing successful African American people on screen. *Within Our Gates* (1920), *Body and Soul* (1925) and *The Girl from Chicago* (1932) were some of his more famous films. Evelyn also became a star. She appeared in many of Oscar Micheaux's films along with other actors such as the good-looking lover-man Lorenzo Tucker, the tough-as-nails Slick Chester, and the towering Paul Robeson.

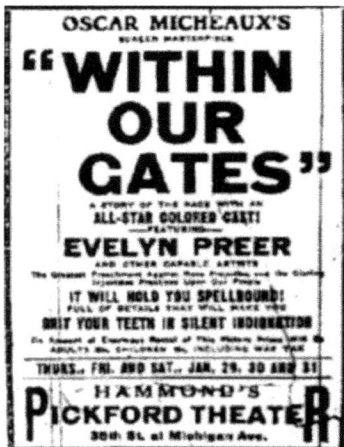

The Gunsaulus Mystery (1921)

The Wages of Sin (1929)

Body and Soul (1925)

MIGHTY MODERN **ALL TALKING** EPIC OF NEGRO LIFE

THE EXILE

Adapted from
"THE CONQUEST"
Written and Directed by
OSCAR MICHEAUX

Distributed by
EMPIRE
723 7th Ave., New York City

The Exile (1931),
Oscar Micheaux's
first all-talking
feature film

The Girl from Chicago (1932)

Veiled Aristocrats (1932)

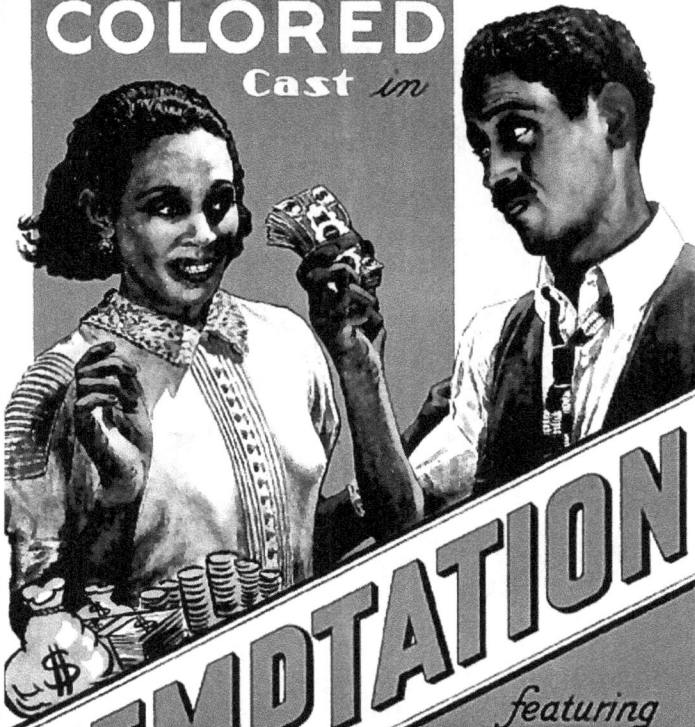

Temptation (1935)

Distributed by MICHEAUX PICTURES CORP NEW YORK CITY

A hot time in the Cotton Club in Micheaux's *Harlem After Midnight* (1934), above, and *Underworld* (1937), left

Swing!
(1938) and
*God's Step
Children*
(1938)

Birthright (1939)

Lying Lips (1939) and *The Notorious Elinor Lee* (1940), both films featured Robert Earl Jones, whose son, James Earl Jones became a mainstream film icon

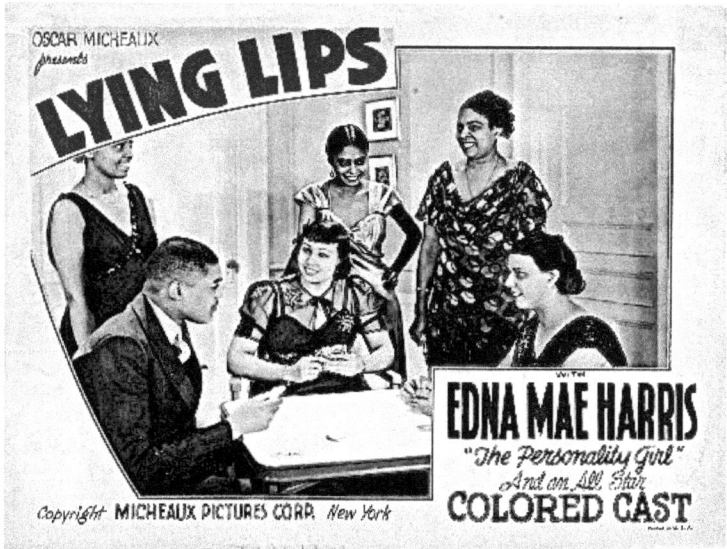

Micheaux's final film, *The Betrayal (1948)*

Books by Oscar Micheaux

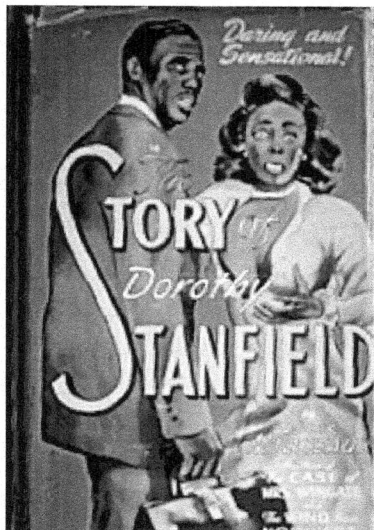

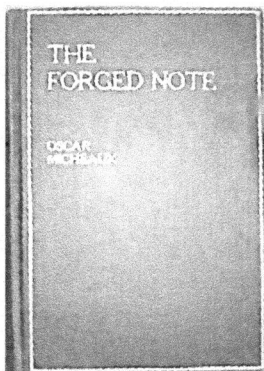

Clockwise from top left, *The Masquerade* published 1947, *The Story of Dorothy Stanfield* published 1946, *The Wind from Nowhere* published 1941, *The Forged Note* published, 1915

In Oscar Micheaux's movies he presented African Americans as doctors, lawyers, teachers and detectives. He wanted to show his people achieving their full potential because he believed that anyone could be anything.

Oscar was not the first black filmmaker. He was not the only black filmmaker. But he had drive and energy and a smooth talking style that few people could match. Between 1919 and 1948 Oscar Micheaux wrote and directed over forty films and seven novels. His movies told positive stories—he believed that anyone could succeed if they took a chance and worked hard. But it wasn't just a story to him. Oscar Micheaux lived that dream. He was a self-made man and his own story showed that anyone could make it no matter what the odds were— even a shoe shiner on a train or a dust covered farmer could be a movie maker.

The Films of Oscar Micheaux

Films directed by Oscar Micheaux:

The Homesteader (1919)

Within Our Gates (1920)

The Brute (1920)

Symbol of the Unconquered (1920)

The Gunsaulus Mystery (1921)

Uncle Jasper's Will (1922)

The Hypocrite (1922)

The Dungeon (1922)

Deceit (1923)

The Virgin of Seminole (1923)

Birthright (1924)

A Son of Satan (1924)

Marcus Garland (1925)

Body and Soul (1925)

The Devil's Disciple (1926)

The Conjure Woman (1926)

The House Behind the Cedars (1927)

The Broken Violin (1927)

The Spider's Web (1927)

The Millionaire (1927)

When Men Betray (1928)

Thirty Years Later (1928)

Wages of Sin (1929)

A Daughter of the Congo (1930)

Easy Street (1930)

Darktown Revue (1931, short film)

The Exile (1931)

The Girl from Chicago (1932)

Black Magic (1932)

Veiled Aristocrats (1932)

Ten Minutes to Live (1932)

Phantom of Kenwood (1933)

Harlem After Midnight (1934)

Temptation (1935)

Murder in Harlem (1935)

Underworld (1937)

Swing! (1938)

God's Step Children (1938)

Birthright (1939)

Lying Lips (1939)

The Notorious Elinor Lee (1940)

The Betrayal (1948)

Books written by Oscar Micheaux:

Conquest: The Story of a Negro Pioneer (1913)

The Forged Note (1915)

The Homesteader: A Novel (1917)

The Wind from Nowhere (1941)

The Case of Mrs. Wingate (1944)

The Story of Dorothy Stanfield (1946)

The Masquerade, a Historical Novel (1947)

African American Filmmakers Making History

For much of film history, movies in America were made by white men. The writers, directors and producers were white. The stars were white. And most audiences were white. When African American people were seen onscreen, their roles were not uplifting or positive. They could only find work as maids, butlers, workers or villains onscreen. While the United States was a mixing pot of diverse cultures, during the Hollywood's Golden Age only one side of the story was seen in movies. This book focuses on the films made by African American filmmakers that were intended for African American audiences. These artists created a separate cinema. They strived to bring a positive messages to their community in their movies.

Burt Williams in *Lime Kiln Club Field Day* (1913)

Operating outside of Hollywood, it took courage, brains and money for African American filmmakers to make movies. Oscar Micheaux (1889-1951) was heroic because he brought a new image of the African American to the screen in more than forty films. In Micheaux's movies, black people struggled but they could rise to become lawyers, doctors and businessmen. Micheaux wanted to show African

American people as successful members of society.

Many of the filmmakers in this story are less well known, obscured by the passage of time. But these less familiar figures are still an important part of film history. Their work brought new voices to the movies.

SEE THE $80,000.00 TRAIN WRECK IN
THE GREEN EYED MONSTER
STUPENDOUS ALL-STAR NEGRO MOTION PICTURE
A BIG SPECIAL PRODUCTION IN EIGHT REELS OF
$1,000,000 RAILROAD EQUIPMENT USED IN THIS PRODUCTION
THRILLS!
ACTION!
PUNCH!
NORMAN FILM MFG. CO.
JACKSONVILLE, FLA.

I. The Pioneers

William D. Foster   *The Green Eyed Monster* (1919)

Oscar Micheaux was an early and important African American filmmaker, but he wasn't the first. The first African American motion picture-maker was William D. Foster (1884-1940). Foster began his career as a journalist. He was a sports writer in Chicago who also worked as an agent for black vaudeville actors.

In 1910 Foster became interested in motion picture production and created the Foster Photoplay Company.

Foster wanted to present African American people in a positive light and break through racial stereotyping. Foster was *the* pioneering black filmmaker. In 1912, he produced a short comedy called *The Railroad Porter*. The next year he made three films: *The Fall Guy* (1913), *The Butler*

A Man's Duty (1919)

(1913), and *The Grafter and the Maid* (1913). With his films in hand, Foster toured the Southern States along the "Chitlin Circuit" of theaters that entertained all-black audiences and introduced his films. Foster set the stage for black filmmakers who would follow after him.

Foster's films were popular because they spoke to their audiences. His films gave African Americans a voice. In these movies, Foster showed the black experience in America onscreen for the first time. This was a different perspective than audiences had seen in *The Birth of a Nation* (1914) and *Uncle Tom's Cabin* (1914). Foster's films inspired other black artists to tell their stories. As his company faded, the Johnson brothers, Noble (1881-1978) and George (1887-1939) stepped up to carry the torch.

George and Noble Johnson
Inspired by the pioneering films of William Forster, George and Noble Johnson created The Lincoln Motion Picture Company in Nebraska in 1915. A year later the brothers opened a studio in Los Angeles. The Lincoln Motion Picture Company, one of the first black film producers, proudly stated its mission as to "encourage black pride." The Johnsons focused on producing uplifting pictures for nearly ten years before the company folded from the pressures of the Great Depression and the expensive transition to sound pictures in late 1920s.

Noble Johnson
in
"The Bronze Bell"
"Serenade"
"Cowtracks"
Now
PRODUCING WESTERNS
with
WESTERN PHOTO PLAY
CORPORATION
LOS ANGELES

Although their production company was gone, the Johnson brothers continued to play an important role in the history of African American film in the U.S. Noble appeared in many Hollywood pictures including *The*

Ten Commandments (1923), *The Thief of Bagdad* (1924), *Moby Dick* (1930), *The Mummy* (1932), *King Kong* (1933) and *She Wore a Yellow Ribbon* (1949). Although these roles were not the uplifting portrayals of African Americans that Noble yearned to bring to the screen, he remained a working actor in Hollywood—appearing in over 140 films—at a time that very few roles were offered to black actors.

Selected films released by The Lincoln Motion Picture Company include: *Trooper of Company K* (1917), *The Law of Nature* (1917), *A Man's Duty* (1919), *By Right of Birth* (1921).

Herb Jeffries
Herb Jeffries was a popular singer before he re-created himself as a crooning cowboy in a series of all-black westerns. In several films Jeffries worked with a young writer-director-performer named Spencer Williams. Williams appeared as a goofy sidekick onscreen but behind the scenes he was a production expert.

Jeffries became known as the "Bronze Buckaroo." He was the African American community's answer to singing cowboys such as Gene Autry and Roy Rogers. Jeffries' low budget westerns included *Harlem on the Prairie* (1937), *Two-Gun Man from Harlem* (1938), *The Bronze Buckaroo* (1939) and *Harlem Rides the Range* (1939). After western films rode off into the sunset, Jeffries' career continued. He made several films in Hollywood, appeared on television and even recorded an album in 1995 called *The Bronze Buckaroo (Rides Again).* In 2013 Jeffries prepares to celebrate his 100th birthday. Herb Jeffries may be the last living link to the race films of African American motion picture history.

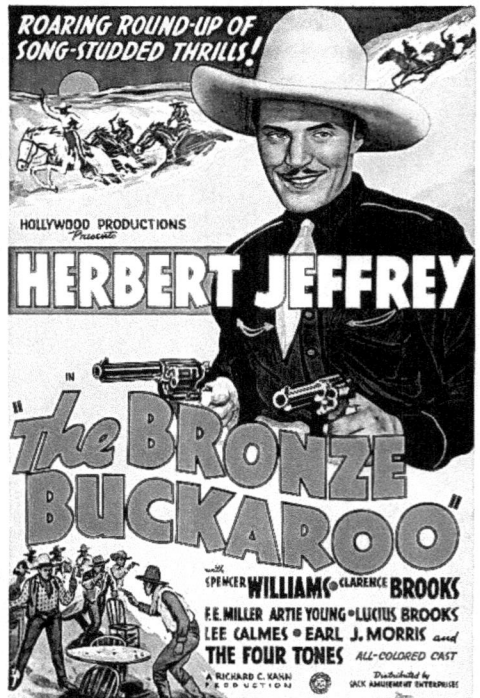

The Bronze Buckaroo (1939)

Spencer Williams

Spencer Williams (1893-1969) appeared with Herb Jeffries in four westerns in the 1930s but Williams' movie career had started before that.

Hired by Al Christie's small movie studio in Hollywood in the late 1920s, Williams learned how to make films on the job. He learned all aspects of the business by working on lighting, assistant directing, writing scripts, acting and doing anything that needed to be done. By 1928 he directed his first film, *Tenderfeet*.

Spencer Williams as Andy in the long running TV series *Amos n' Andy*

Now that Williams knew the business inside and out, in 1931 he opened his own movie and newsreel company called The Lincoln Talking Pictures Company. Producing films on shoestring budgets, Williams was able to direct *The Blood of Jesus*

(1941), *Go Down, Death!* (1944) and *Dirty Gertie from Harlem U.S.A.* (1944). In the 1950s, Williams took a steady job as Amos on the television show *Amos 'n Andy* to support his independent motion picture projects.

Williams is an interesting figure—he worked to bring an independent African American voice to the screen but also contributed to racial stereotypes in his most famous role. Williams was a filmmaker caught between ideals and reality at a time when working in the motion picture industry was nearly to impossible for any minority.

II. Working in the Studio System

Working in the Hollywood studio system could be challenging for any performer but the difficulty was multiplied for African American actors during the Golden Age of Hollywood. Several actresses stood out to make a lasting impression: Hattie MacDaniel, Ethel Waters and Lena Horne.

Hatte MacDaniel

Hattie McDaniel (1892-1952) mostly portrayed maids, but a maid played by Hattie always seemed to run the show and rule the roost. She donned the traditional black and white uniform in *Blonde Venus* (1933) to serve Marlene Dietrich, she catered to Mae West in *I'm No Angel* (1933) and helped make Katharine Hepburn's big date a success in *Alice Adams* (1935). McDaniel also appeared in some of Hollywood's biggest productions, such as *Showboat* (1936) and her most famous role as Mammy in *Gone with the Wind* (1939).

Hattie MacDaniel won an Academy Award for Best Supporting Actress in *Gone with the Wind*—she was the first African American performer to ever claim the award. But when the film premiered in Atlanta, she wasn't permitted to attend the show because she was black. Clark Gable threatened to boycott the premiere but Hattie insisted that he go. Hattie MacDaniel blazed new trails but was also trapped in a traditional order. She could win awards but she couldn't change the attitudes of her day.

Ethel Waters

Ethel Waters (1896-1977) was a top singer and performer on the vaudeville circuit, playing on stages to adoring crowds around the country before she ever appeared in a film. She was one of the highest paid actresses on Broadway when MGM lured her to Hollywood to appear in the all-black extravaganza *Cabin in the Sky* (1943). In *Cabin*, Waters dominated the screen as a strong woman fighting for her weak-willed husband's soul (played by Eddie "Rochester" Anderson). Eddie is tempted when the devil sends a beautiful woman, personified by Lena Horne, to destroy his marriage. Ethel wasn't scared by either Lena or the Devil as she fought to win her husband back. Ten years later Ethel Waters was nominated for Academy Award for *Pinky* (1949).

Lena Horne appeared with Ralph Cooper in *The Duke is Tops* aka *The Bronze Venus* (1938)

Lena Horne

Lena Horne (1917-2010) presents one of the more tragic stories in African American film history. She was beautiful, talented, and bursting with star power. But she was black. Because of that, Hollywood struggled to find a role for her. When she did appear in a movie, it was usually in role that could be cut out for films sent to theaters in the Southern States. Horne was a successful and award winning Broadway actress and singer but her career in movies was held up by racial issues in Hollywood and America.

III. Breaking Through

Hattie MacDaniel and Ethel Waters built solid film careers during the Golden Age of Hollywood. But Sidney Poitier, Gordon Parks and Spike Lee broke through barriers for African Americans in mainstream Hollywood films.

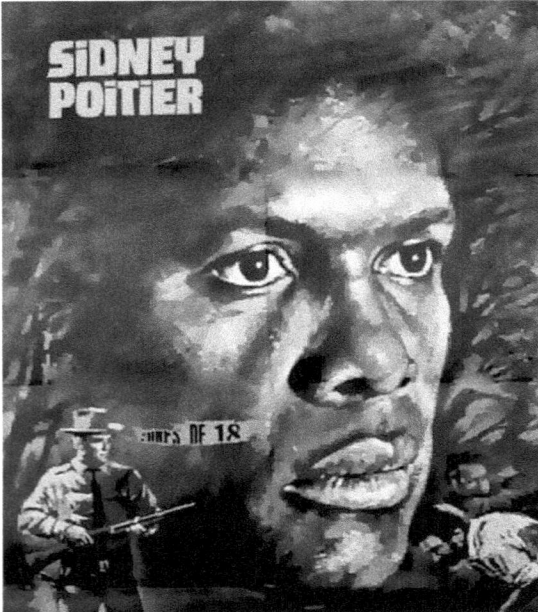

Sidney Poitier

Poitier appeared in *No Way Out* (1950) not as a butler, farm worker or native but as a medical doctor. This was an important moment for African American actors in Hollywood. Forced to confront racism at his hospital, Poitier's character shows his inner strength and proves that his value has no relation to his skin

Poitier continued playing strong men of conviction in films such as *Something of Value (1957), The Defiant Ones (1958)* and *A Raisin in the Sun (1961). Poitier* claimed his Academy Award—the first African American man to be named Best Actor—for *Lilies of the Field (1963).* His powerful performances continued in *A Patch of Blue (1965)* and *In the Heat of the Night (1967).*

While Poitier was a leading man in front of the camera, Gordon Parks broke through equally difficult barriers behind the scenes.

Gordon Parks Sr.

Gordon Parks (1912-2006) began his career as a writer and photographer for *Life Magazine.* By 1969 he became the first African American to direct a major Hollywood motion picture. Parks had written an autobiography entitled *The Learning Tree* then directed the film adaptation for Warner Bros.

Richard Roundtree in *Shaft's Big Score* (1972)

Following his life story, Parks launched a new genre—blaxploitation—when he made *Shaft* (1971). Shaft, played by Richard Roundtree, was a black super-detective that crossed color lines to become hugely popular. Like Poitier, Parks made movies that could reach mainstream audiences.

Spike Lee

Ten years later Spike Lee (b. 1957) led a new generation of African American filmmakers. In *She's Gotta Have It* (1986), Spike created a world of quirky characters that shared the same problems as other young people: a girl looked for love, a boy obsessed over the New York Knicks. Even though Spike brought black voices to the screen, everyone could relate to his movies. *Do the Right Thing* (1989) and *Malcolm X* (1992) showed difficult moments in the African American experience but were seen and appreciated by all audiences.

Since the days of Oscar Micheaux, the Johnson brothers and Spencer Williams, American movies have evolved and developed. Filmmakers like

Poitier, Parks and Lee brought diverse themes to the screen and made interesting and important films that could speak to and enrich all audiences.

While African American performers were once restricted to race films, now black actors can headline summer blockbusters. Samuel L. Jackson commanded *The Avengers*. The names Will Smith, Eddie Murphy and Idris Elba are often printed above the title. But without a doubt the most memorable performer in the biggest blockbuster was James Earl Jones.

James Earl Jones first gained attention in *The Great White Hope* (1970) but it was as the booming baritone voice of Darth Vader in *Star Wars* (1977) that Jones became one of the most recognizable performers in all of film history.

Jones grew up in the movie community. His father, Robert Earl Jones (1910-2006) began his film career acting in several of Oscar Micheaux's films, including *Lying Lips* (1939). In one generation,

James Earl Jones was able to witness firsthand how black actors emerged from race films to star in studio tentpole productions.

The story of the African American experience in film is not a just a history but a continuing, unfolding and evolving tale. New, different and diverse voices in the movies create a fuller and more inspiring experience for all audiences.

This brief history of African American contributions to film history does not tell the complete story. There are many more great talents. There are more powerful performers including Paul Robeson and Josephine Baker, Louise Beavers, Rex Ingram, Nina Mae McKinney, Dorothy Dandridge and Harry Belefonte, Ossie Davis and Ruby Dee, Clarence Muse and Oscar Polk. Current filmmakers include the tireless Tyler Perry, the versatile Ernest Dickerson and many more emerging actors, directors, writers, musicians, animators and film crew-members who have not yet had their chance to shine.

IV. Recognition

From the 1920s-1960s Hollywood movies presented the world according to a white male voice. But through much effort, diverse talents began to emerge onscreen. African American performers and craftspeople broke through barriers and were soon recognized with Hollywood's highest achievements. These performers were celebrated not because they were African American, but because they were truly great talents.

Academy Award Winners for
Best Actor in a Leading Role
Sidney Poitier, *Lilies of the Field* (1963)
Denzel Washington, *Training Day* (2001)
Jamie Foxx, *Ray* (2004)
Forest Whitaker, *The Last King of Scotland* (2006)

Academy Award Winner for
Best Actress in a Leading Role
Halle Berry, *Monster's Ball* (2001)

Academy Award Winners for
Best Actor in a Supporting Role
Louis Gossett, Jr., *An Officer and a Gentleman* (1982)
Denzel Washington, *Glory* (1989)
Cuba Gooding, Jr. *Jerry Maguire* (1996)
Morgan Freeman, *Million Dollar Baby* (2004)

Academy Award Winners for
Best Actress in a Supporting Role
Hattie MacDaniel, *Gone with the Wind* (1939)
Whoopie Goldberg, *Ghost* (1990)
Jennifer Hudson, *Dreamgirls* (2006)
Mo'Nique, *Precious* (2009)
Octavia Spencer, *The Help* (2011)

Academy Award Nominees for
Best Actor in a Leading Role
Sidney Poitier, *The Defiant Ones* (1958)
James Earl Jones, *The Great White Hope* (1970)
Paul Winfield, *Sounder* (1972)
Dexter Gordon, *Round Midnight* (1986)
Laurence Fishburne, *What's Love Got to Do with It* (1993)
Morgan Freeman, *The Shawshank Redemption* (1994)
Denzel Washington, *The Hurricane* (1999)
Will Smith, *Ali* (2001)
Don Cheadle, *Hotel Rwanda* (2004)
Terence Howard, *Hustle & Flow* (2005)
Will Smith, *The Pursuit of Happyness* (2006)
Morgan Freeman, *Invictus* (2009)
Denzel Washington, *Flight* (2012)

Academy Award Nominees for
Best Actress in a Leading Role
Dorothy Dandridge, *Carmen Jones* (1954)
Diana Ross, *Lady Sings the Blues* (1972)
Cicely Tyson, *Sounder* (1972)
Diahann Carroll, *Claudine* (1974)
Whoopie Goldberg, *The Color Purple* (1985)
Angela Bassett, *What's Love Got to Do with It* (1993)
Gabourey Sidbe, *Precious* (2009)
Viola Davis, *The Help* (2011)
Quvenzhane Wallis, *Beasts of the Southern Wild* (2012)

Academy Award Nominees for
Best Actor in a Supporting Role
Rupert Crosse, *The Reivers* (1969)
Howard Rollins, *Ragtime* (1981)
Adolph Caesar, *A Soldier's Story* (1984)
Morgan Freeman, *Street Smart* (1987)
Denzel Washington, *Cry Freedom* (1987)
Jaye Davidson, *The Crying Game* (1992)
Samuel L. Jackson, *Pulp Fiction* (1994)
Michael Clarke Duncan, *The Green Mile* (1999)
Djimon Hounsou, *In America* (2003)
Jamie Foxx, *Collateral* (2004)
Djimon Hounsou, *Blood Diamond* (2006)
Eddie Murphy, *Dreamgirls* (2006)

Academy Award Nominees for
Best Actress in a Supporting Role
Ethel Waters, *Pinky* (1949)
Juanita Moore, *Imitation of Life* (1959)
Beah Richards, *Guess Who's Coming to Dinner* (1967)
Alfre Woodard, *Cross Creek* (1983)
Oprah Winfrey, *The Color Purple* (1985)
Marianne Jean-Baptiste, *Secrets & Lies* (1996)
Queen Latifah, *Chicago* (2002)
Sophie Okonedo, *Hotel Rwanda* (2004)
Ruby Dee, *American Gangster* (2007)
Viola Davis, *Doubt* (2008)
Taraji P. Henson, *The Curious Case of Benjamin Button*
(2008)

Academy Award Nominees for Direction
John Singleton, *Boyz n the Hood* (1991)
Lee Daniels, *Precious* (2009)

Academy Award Nominee for Cinematography
Remi Adefarasin, *Elizabeth* (1998)

Academy Award Nominee for Editing
Hugh A. Robertson, *Midnight Cowboy* (1969)

Academy Award Nominees for
Writing (Original Screenplay)
Suzanne de Passe, *Lady Sings the Blues* (1972)
Spike Lee, *Do the Right Thing* (1989)
John Singleton, *Boyz n the Hood* (1991)

Academy Award Nominees for
Writing (Adapted Screenplay)
Lonnie Elder, *Sounder* (1972)
Charles Fuller, *A Soldier's Story* (1984)

Academy Award Nominees for Costume Design
Ruth E. Carter, *Malcolm X* (1992)
Ruth E. Carter, *Amistad* (1997)
Sharen Davis, *Ray* (2004)
Sharen Davis, *Dreamgirls* (2006)

Academy Award Winners for Best Score
Prince, *Purple Rain* (1984)
Herbie Hancock, *Round Midnight* (1986)

Academy Award Nominees for Best Score
Duke Ellington, *Paris Blues* (1961)
Quincy Jones, *In Cold Blood* (1967)
Isaac Hayes, *Shaft* (1971)
Quincy Jones, *The Wiz* (1978)
Quincy Jones, Andrae Crouch and Caiphus Semenya,
The Color Purple (1985)
Jonas Gwangwa, *Cry Freedom* (1987)

Academy Award Winners for Best Original Song
Isaac Hayes, "Theme from Shaft" from *Shaft* (1971)
Irene Cara, "Flashdance (What a Feeling)" from *Flash-dance* (1983)
Stevie Wonder, "I Just Called to Say I Love You" from
The Woman in Red (1984)
Lionel Ritchie, "Say You, Say Me" from *White Nights* (1985)
Juicy J, Frayser Boy and DJ Paul, "It's Hard Out Here for a Pimp" from *Hustle & Flow* (2005)

Academy Award Nominees for Original Song
Quincy Jones and Bob Russell, "The Eyes of Love" from *Banning* (1967)
Quincy Jones and Bob Russell, "For Love of Ivy" from *For Love of Ivy* (1968)
Lionel Ritchie, "Endless Love" from *Endless Love* (1981)
Ray Parker, Jr., "Ghostbusters" from *Ghostbusters* (1984)
Quincy Jones, Lionel Ritchie, and Rod Temperton, "Miss Celie's Blues" from *The Color Purple* (1985)
Jonas Gwangwa, "Cry Freedom" from *Cry Freedom* (1987)
Jimmy Jam, Terry Lewis and Janet Jackson, "Again" from *Poetic Justice* (1993)
James Ingram, "The Day I Fall in Love" from *Beethoven's 2nd* (1993)
James Ingram, "Look What Love Has Done" from *Junior* (1995)
Siedah Garrett, "Love You I Do" from *Dreamgirls* (2006)
Jamal Joseph, Charles Mack and Tevin Thomas, "Raise It Up" from *August Rush* (2007)
Siedah Garrett, "Real in Rio" from *Rio* (2011)

Academy of Motion Pictures Arts and Sciences
Special Honors

James Baskett received special recognition for his
role as Uncle Remus in *Song of the South* (1948)

Quincy Jones received the Jean Hersholt
Humanitarian Award (1995)

Sidney Poitier received an Honorary Award (2002)

James Earl Jones received an Honorary Award (2011)

Oprah Winfrey received the Jean Hersholt
Humanitarian Award (2011)

IV. Preserving African American Film History

In 1988 the United States Congress acted to preserve the Nation's motion picture heritage by passing a law that created the National Film Preservation Board. Each year since 1988 twenty- five films are selected to be celebrated and preserved with distinction in the National Film Registry. Several culturally significant landmarks of black cinema have been selected for this high honor.

Within Our Gates (1920): directed by Oscar Micheaux.

St. Louis Blues (1929): this short film features a rare and valuable performance by singer Bessie Smith.

The Emperor Jones (1933): adapted from Eugene O'Neill's stage play, *The Emperor Jones* stars Paul Robeson in one of his finest performances.

Imitation of Life (1934): produced by Universal Pictures, *Imitation* featured Louise Beavers and Claudette Colbert in a sensitive story of the friendship between women that looks past racial issues.

Showboat (1936): this major production produced by Universal Pictures featured Hattie MacDaniel and Paul Robeson, who sang his memorable version of "Ol' Man River."

The Nicholas Brothers Family Home Movies (1930s-1940s): although never commercially released, this documentary contains footage of the dancing duo as they perform their signature acrobatic and athletic moves at the Cotton Club in Harlem and on the Broadway stage.

The Blood of Jesus (1941): Spencer Williams' heartfelt personal film opens a window on a bygone era.

Stormy Weather (1943): a who's who of African American screen stars with Lena Horne, Cab Calloway, Bill "Bojangles" Robinson, the Nicholas brothers, Fats Waller and other great performers.

Carmen Jones (1954): a rare example of a Hollywood studio film that featured an all black cast. Produced by 20th Century Fox, *Carmen Jones* starred the beautiful Dorothy Dandridge with Harry Belefonte, Pearl Bailey, Dihann Carroll and Brock Peters.

Porgy and Bess (1959): based on the Gershwin opera, directed by Otto Preminger and produced by Columbia Pictures. *Porgy* features Sidney Poitier, Dorothy Dandridge and Sammy Davis Jr., with an unforgettable soundtrack.

A Raisin in the Sun (1961): adapted from the classic stage play, Columbia Pictures' *Raisin* features Sidney Poitier, Ruby Dee and Lou Gossett Jr.

Nothing But a Man (1964): an independent film set in the deep South, this picture starred Ivan Dixon. While Dixon might not be as well known as Poitier or Spike Lee, Dixon acted and directed in film and television consistently from 1970-1994, a rare feat for an African American talent.

In the Heat of the Night (1967): this Academy Award winning film celebrated the inner strength and bravery of Sidney Poitier against crushing Southern racism. With his famous line: "They Call me *Mister* Tibbs," Poitier boldly stood up to Rod Steiger's racist law man. In addition to winning five Academy Awards, *In the Heat of the Night* inspired two sequels, *They Call Me MISTER Tibbs* (1970) and *The Organization* (1971) as well as a television series (1988-1992).

The Learning Tree (1969): this sensitive coming of age story was based on Gordon Parks Sr.'s autobiography. *The Learning Tree* was the first film directed by an African American filmmaker that was funded by a major motion pictures studio (Warner Bros.).

King: A Filmed Record...Montgomery to Memphis (1970): this documentary captured important moments in the Civil Rights movement with footage of Dr. Martin Luther King Jr.'s life from the 1955 bus boycott to his assassination thirteen years later.

Shaft (1971): Gordon Park Sr.'s stylish film popularized the blaxploitation genre and featured Richard Roundtree as a fearless, smart and sexy detective. Isaac Hayes funky score won an Academy Award for the theme song.

Killer of Sheep (1977): Charles Burnett's fiercely independent   production tells the story of an African American man's difficult existence working in a slaughterhouse. Despite a limited release, *Killer of Sheep* built a passionate following.

Michael Jackson's *Thriller* music video (1983). The King of Pop changed the musical landscape with his epic horror film-music video-dance extravaganza. With zombies, moonwalking and great choreography—this video could never be equaled.

Do the Right Thing (1989): Spike Lee's passionate look at racial disharmony on a incendiary summer day in Brooklyn. This drama spoke to people across race lines; it was a film that everyone in America had to see and talk about.

Boyz N the Hood (1991): filled with heartfelt moments about a boy forever connected to his neighborhood even as he tries to better his life. Director John Singleton made this film when he was 24 years old and went on to become the youngest person—of any race—to win a Best Director Academy Award.

Daughters of the Dust (1991): the first movie directed by an African American woman to be released in theaters nation-wide, Julie Dash's labor of love took ten years to produce. Focusing on the isolated Gullah culture of the South Carolina barrier islands, Dash's film has been celebrated for its story, her research and dazzling cinematography.

Malcolm X (1992): Spike Lee followed up to *Do the Right Thing* was an even more uncompromising film based on the life of the controversial Civil Rights activist, played by Denzel Washington.

Hoop Dreams (1994): this riveting documentary focuses on two students who have great aspirations to build a better life by relying on their athletic abilities.   Five years of filming presents great triumphs as well as devastating setbacks in a realistic picture of inner city youths.

Conclusion

Wallace Worsley directing Rhea Mitchell in Social Ambition (1918)

The lights go down. The curtains open. An image flickers to life on screen as we enter another world for two hours.

In this new world superheroes can defend the Earth from intergalactic and mutant villains. In this screen world a femme fatale can control a man with one smoldering pouty glance. In this fantasy world comedians can drive a car off a cliff and walk away unharmed.

We love the movies because they can transport us to thrilling and glamorous dream lands. The movies show us stories that can change our lives—or at least escape from them for a short time.

But the stories behind the screen can be equally dramatic. The men, women, boys, and girls that made the movies can provide inspiring stories of success. Talents like Charlie Chaplin, Greta Garbo and Oscar Micheaux struggled to create a better life. With unwavering will power they made their dreams a reality—and they became screen legends. By reading their stories we can remind ourselves never to give up on our dreams and aspirations no matter how far away they may seem.

In the movies, anything is always possible.

There are plenty more stories to tell
from *Behind the Screen.*

Discover more great books on film at
Hollywood-Press.com !

The End

www.ingramcontent.com/pod-product-compliance
Lightning Source LLC
Chambersburg PA
CBHW070552030426
42337CB00016B/2461